Pictures of Victorian Ashford and District

from Ashford Borough Museum Society's

Collection of Photographs

Published by Geerings of Ashford Ltd.

Front Cover photograph:
The Ashford Bank taken over by Lloyds Bank and rebuilt.
Absence of traffic enables the boys to pose for the photographer.

Introduction

The photographs reproduced in this book have been selected from an album containing over 500 pictures of Ashford and some nearby villages, taken in the last quarter of the nineteenth century.

The album was dedicated on the fly-leaf to 'Thomas Barns, from Polly, 1891'. We have some information gleaned from parish records and directories about the Barns family. Thomas was born in 1833 and was one of four sons of James and Ann Barns. James was a cabinet maker and traded at 6 Middle Row, Ashford. The family traded in a variety of skills, as will be seen from the advertisements reproduced here from the 'Kentish Express' of May 7th, 1864.

Another photographer in Ashford about this time was Thomas Kingsmill, trading at 100 High Street in 1859 and later at 2 George Street (now Bank Street). A brother of Thomas Barns, Samuel West Barnes, another photographer, traded at 100 High Street in 1874. In the early part of this century until the late 1940's this shop was run by Hugh Penfold, another photographer, thus carrying on the tradition in the same premises.

As the Barns brothers were all photographers it is not clear precisely who took the photographs in the album. This is further complicated by the fact that some of the photographs are stated to be from 'Kingsmill negatives'. However, whoever did take the pictures was not only a good photographer with an eye for composition, but also a possessor of excellent equipment.

The pictures in the album generally carry a reference number, some of which have the prefix Sterio *(sic)*. This shows that the photographs were produced in duplicate for viewing with a stereoscope. These were popular items at the time and many specimens still survive. Viewed through the two eyepieces, the photographs take on a 3/D effect. It will be noted that the advertisements shown above refer to views for the stereoscope.

The Ashford Borough Museum Society commissioned the work of enlarging and improving the photographs in the album, which now present a valuable record of the town of Ashford and the villages of Appledore, Biddenden, Bilsington, Brabourne, Great Chart (including Godinton House and Park) and Little Chart (including Calehill Park).

A number of the photographs in the album have over the years been accidentally exposed to ultra-violet light causing fading and discolourisation. In many cases much of this was minimized by the expertise of Mr. W. L. Entwistle, a professional photographer of Canterbury, who took a great personal interest in the project.

The photographs are described by Walter Briscall, who acknowledges the assistance given by Richard Filmer. Thanks are also due to Arthur Ruderman for supplying details of the Barns family.

Ashford

The town possesses one of the widest High Streets, at least in Kent — a relic of its Anglo-Saxon origin. In the middle Ages it is thought that it was even wider, as the southern side dates mainly from the 18th century.

Although by the late 19th century this market town had an infusion of industry by the Railway Works, the High Street scenes that follow are those of quiet simplicity with little vehicular traffic and few pedestrians — just a few hand-carts and barrows. No doubt Barns with the slow speed film of the day chose moments of quietness to record the scenes.

Ashford Lower High Street from East Hill. The grocer's shop was at the corner of High Street and Wellesley Road, formerly Gravel Pit Street. Note the biscuit tins in the doorway. The iron posts in front of several shops were supports for shop blinds.

Lower High Street Ashford South Side

The south side of lower High Street. Williamson's, 13 and 15 is in the 1980s occupied by a food shop and an ironmonger's.

The south side of lower High Street showing the 'Royal Oak Hotel'. Note the carrier who served Lydd and Folkestone. All the buildings seen here have been demolished.

The Royal Oak Hotel in lower High Street was an ancient hostelry with an eighteenth-century frontage. At one time a corn market was held here. The building was demolished to make way for the Pearl Assurance block.

The building occupied by Wells and J. U. Bugler was demolished in 1935/6 and an Odeon Cinema built, now 'Top Rank' Bingo Hall. Note the splendid street gas lamp.

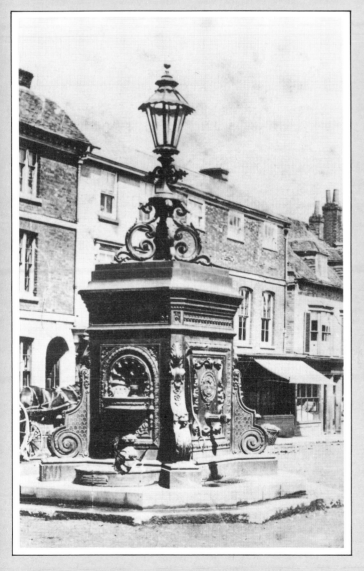

This is a fine photograph of the Drinking Fountain presented to the town in 1864 by Robert Furley, solicitor and historian. His son was Sir John Furley of St. John Ambulance fame. The fountain stood on the site of the old town pump.

Lower High Street Ashford North Side

(a)

(a) The London and County Bank, now the National Westminster Bank. This was demolished and the present building erected.

(b) Mr. Thorpe's draper's shop at the corner of High Street and North Street. Note the Ionic columns. The white strip in the road was a 'pedestrian' crossing, kept clear of horse droppings by a 'crossing sweeper' (for a consideration no doubt).

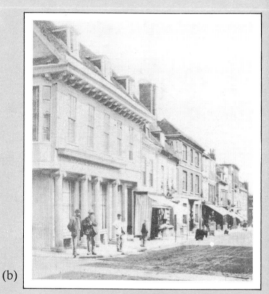
(b)

(c)

(c) The shops in lower High Street have been decorated for the Duke of Edinburgh's Reception, The Duke leased Eastwell Park in 1878 for twenty years.

Middle Row
Ashford

The east end of Middle Row with the Drinking Fountain. The door entered a passage between the two buildings which now join to make a single shop.

Thompson's shop in Middle Row (Part seen in the photograph below Granny Rabsons). The building is possibly Ashford's oldest and was restored in 1982 when it was occupied by an estate agency.

Thompson's shop and 'Granny Rabsons'. Thompson was a jeweller, silversmith and printer. The Rabson family started trading in the town in 1720. Note that the shop at the corner of North Street had no windows at that time in North Street.

7

The wide lower High Street has been brought to a halt with the Middle Row cluster of buildings, thus creating narrow parts to the north and south. The northern section could be described as the nucleus of the town – the point where the old way from Canterbury or Faversham enters the town. North Street (or North Lane as it was called in earlier days) became part of the turnpike road which here turned eastwards down the High Street towards Hythe through Willesborough.

North Street. This looks towards the High Street. The present Masonic Hall is on the left with the pillared doorway. Further on the Red Lion Inn sports its projecting sign. Later on its name was changed to The Lord Roberts of Boer War fame only to be demolished to make Park Street East. Note the gas lamp standard and the lady in characteristic Victorian dress.

On the left of the picture there is the clock on Thompson's shop and a projecting gas lamp. The canopy, which also supports a gas lamp, became the favourite place from which parliamentary candidates harangued the public.

Further up the street the competing George Commercial Hotel boasts a hanging sign suspended from an ornate cast iron bracket. The sign states that W. J. Davis is the proprietor.

A few humble buildings on the corner of North Street were demolished and the Saracen's Head was expanded up to the corner. The hotel had developed from a coaching inn in order to cater for the commercial travellers who came to the town by the new railway. A horse bus plied between the hotel and the station.

West of Middle Row and Upper High Street

The west end of the Middle Row group of shops showing Crust's the butcher's. Note that the tall building which is now part of the 'Man of Kent' public house has elegant sun-blinds to the first floor windows. The floral decorations to the shops seems to indicate some celebration.

The north side of High Street. At left of centre the hanging sign is at the George Hotel. Then to the right, an outfitter (Taylor about 1850-90), a grocer (Spain about 1870-95) and a hairdresser (Gore about 1854-91). These shops were demolished for Marks & Spencer before they moved to upper High Street.

Upper High Street

Scott's House, one of two 17th-century houses, was destroyed by fire. Later the site of both houses was redeveloped.

The building at the corner of Bank Street was The Ashford Bank, which later became Lloyds who rebuilt the premises in the 1920s. This is an interesting picture with its group of boys, the carriage and the long-skirted lady standing beside it. Absence of traffic gave the photographer an excellent opportunity.

This picture shows part of the north side of the former Assembly Rooms. Part of the building was used as accommodation for the Fire Engine and Fire Brigade's equipment.

The baker's shop on the left was the site of the Entrance and Balcony of the Urban Council's Offices which were erected in 1925. This centre block, formerly the Assembly Rooms, is now occupied by shops and known as King's Parade. The corner building on the right was the Ashford Bank, later demolished and rebuilt for Lloyds Bank.

The north side of the upper High Street. Number 80, Millers' became Geerings. The low building to the left is now Clouds. These are the only two buildings still standing. J. Chittenden had a variety of occupations, Auctioneer, appraiser, new and second-hand furniture and a bedding and mattress manufactory.

More Upper High Street

Norley's Stationer's Shop was at 95A High Street – now occupied by part of the Tufton Centre and opposite the entrance to the Park Mall precinct. In 1910 the shop became Geerings.

Upper High Street 'as of old'. The high building on the left was a new store for Lewis & Hyland, next to which was 'The Fountain' inn, a commodious hostelry. Note Brothers' chemist's shop, later Gutteridge's, all now gone for modern developments.

The lettering on the sign reads as follows:

NORLEY

Agent for the BEST AMERICAN & ENGLISH SEWING MACHINES

———

Free trial at Home Before Purchase No Deposit required Payments taken Weekly or Monthly Without extra charge. Full discount allowed if paid Within One Month after Purchase. Kept in repair 12 Months without Charge. INSTRUCTIONS FREE Ask for Price List & Special Terms

———

MACHINES KEPT FOR HIRE 95 HIGH ST.

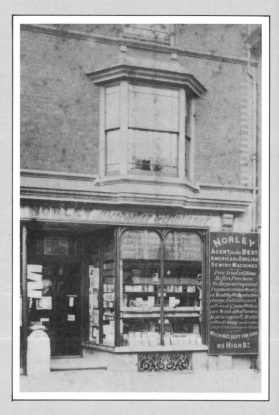

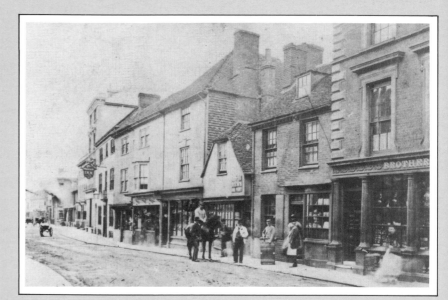

More Upper High Street

High Street showing Norley's shop, later Geering's before the firm moved across the road. Lewis & Hyland's and Norley's have now made way for part of the Tufton Centre.

This photograph shows George Harper's furniture store at 8-10 Castle Street. It was he who presented the Fountain, formerly in Olantigh Park, Wye, now in Victoria Park, to the town.

Next door was the basket stores of John Harper, an uncle of George. All these premises have now gone with the building of the Park Mall development.

Usborne and Worger's shop was in New Street next to the Old Prince of Wales public house.

Bank Street

The entrance to Bank Street was originally a garden belonging to the old Ashford Bank, and its continuation then called George Street opened the way to the creation of a new Cattle Market. The surveyor Thomas Thurston drew up his grand plan for the Jemmetts to make Elwick Road which he intended to continue onto Godinton Road but that was not carried out until the modern Ringway was made.

Bank Street looking north towards the High Street. The gap in the street where tree is, was later filled in by the Masonic Hall, and again became a gap when the Tufton Centre was built.

The Masonic Hall in Bank Street built in multi-coloured brickwork was next to the present branch of the National Provincial Bank but has now been demolished.

George Street was at first the name given to the lower part of the present Bank Street, after George Elwick Jemmett, the lord of the manor. The shop on the left became the offices of Alfred J. Burrows, surveyor. Nichols next door was a printer, stationer and paperbag manufacturer.

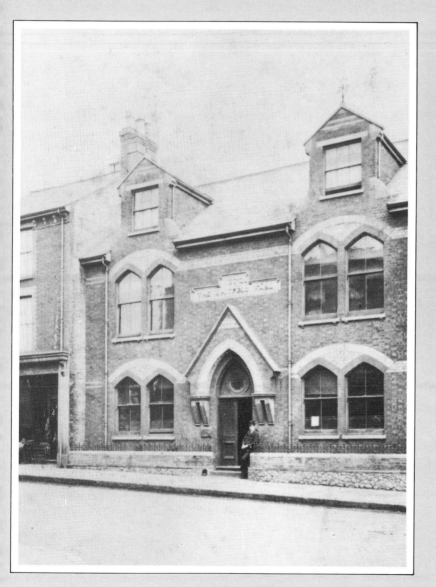

The Whitfeld Hall in Bank Street still stands but converted into hairdressing saloons. The hall was built in 1874 by a local builder, Wood, and named after a prominent Ashford citizen, Henry Whitfeld. (N.B. not Whitfield).

Bank Street

This picture was taken at the junction of Tufton Street and Bank Street, looking towards the lower part of the present Bank Street, then called George Street. Kingsmill the photographer, mentioned in the Introduction, had a shop at No. 2 George Street, shown here at the corner with photographs in the window.

This is a better view of the Post Office in Bank Street which has lost its clock and later became the National Provincial Bank.
The building with the clock was the Post Office.

The photographer describes this as the 'Board School' − an obvious mistake. The picture shows the almshouses, formerly in Tufton Street opposite the present Post Office, erected on land given by G. E. Jemmett. The cost of the almshouses was defrayed partly by public subscription and partly from a legacy of James Wall. (The latter sold land to the South Eastern Railway Company).

The Corn Exchange with its imposing entrance as originally built in 1861. Later the portico was taken down and the entrance moved so that a stage could be built at that end. Trafalgar House now occupies the site.

The interior of the Corn Exchange as a Ballroom. This was the scene of many concerts, dances and theatrical performances. On market days the scene changed to one of commercial activity with Corn Merchants displaying their samples and no doubt haggling over prices.

The Market Hotel was built after the cattle market moved from lower High Street. It is now called the 'Wig and Gavel'. Next to it, until recently stood the premises of Stanhay Limited, motor and agricultural engineers.

Ashford Church

The Church tower has dominated the landscape for over 500 years. Sir John Fogge of Repton enlarged the church and built the tower in 1475. His tomb chest stands beside the high altar and his heavy tilting helmet, known in heraldic terms as his helm, hangs on the north wall near his tomb.

(a)

(a) The Parish Church as seen from the old burial ground at the corner of Vicarage Lane and Station Road, (now laid out as a public garden). It will be noted that the church tower has no clock face. This dates the photograph before 1885. The factory with the chimney stack was Bugler's Iron Foundry, later G. M. Mather.

(b) The Parish Church seen from Miss Cook's. Miss Cook had a restaurant at 51-53 High Street which backs onto the Church Yard. This photograph again pre-dates 1885 when the big old clock was replaced.

(b)

(c)

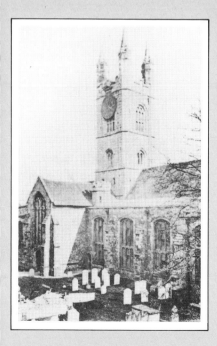

Ashford Church

(c) The pinnacles of the church tower are faintly seen behind the Victorian addition to the so-called Clergy House. The addition was built by a Mr. Rabson. It is interesting to note that the iron gates to the churchyard were probably made in the Ashford Foundry.

This is a view of the Church and The College. The brick exterior of the latter conceals the 15th century wing. Many of the trees have now gone.

The Parish Church interior. This view shows the more open view without the present screen. The old reredos behind the high altar and the old-fashioned box pews have been replaced.

This is another view of the Church as seen from the Grammar School Master's house (since demolished). The wooden clockface was put up in 1688.

Ashford Grammar School

This is one of the gables of the house of the headmaster of the old Ashford Grammar School. The house adjoined the school room which is now called the Doctor Wilks' Hall. The house was demolished at the end of the last century.

The Church Yard looking towards the old Grammar School and the Master's house. The cast-iron railings were made at the Ashford Foundry of Dungey in 1838. Later, Dungey's became Bugler's and then Mather's, one of the oldest firms in Ashford.

The upper part of the Grammar School Master's house next to the School. The house was demolished when the High Street shops were built.

(a)

In its history there had always been influential non-conformists in the town. A number of successful traders belonged to non-conformist bodies. There were members of the Society of Friends in Ashford in 1688 and before that there was a Baptist congregation.

(a) The Friends' Meeting House was built in 1802 on ground between the windmill and New Rents. Later Lewis & Hyland's store was built in front — part of the store may be seen on the right.

(b)

(b) The Wesleyan Chapel, Hempstead Street. After the Wesleyans built a new church in Bank Street, this became the Friends' Meeting House. It was later demolished during the Tufton Street development.

(c)

(c) The Congregational Church was at the corner of Tufton Street and Church Road, demolished when the new Magistrates' Courts were built.

Church Road

The Particular Baptist Chapel was built in Norwood Street in 1863. Later it was called the 'Ebenezer Chapel' and was demolished when the Police Headquarters were built.

Stoke House, Church Road, was the home of J. U. Bugler, the ironmonger of High Street, with an iron foundry at the rear, all on the site of the present Top Rank building. Stoke House stood at the corner of Norwood Street where part of the Police Headquarters has been built. Note the elaborate railings — no doubt made at Bugler's Foundry.

Church Villas in Church Road are seen from across the Glebe Land, which later became the Memorial Gardens after the 1914-18 war. On the extreme left, the two houses were bombed in the last war. The Library was built on the site.

New Street replaced the old way into the town through Gravel Walk and New Rents. This new road was part of the turnpike highway from both Maidstone and Biddenden in the 18th century. This opened for some residential and shopping development – including a number of public houses. Note the rough condition of the road.

This photograph shows the 'British Volunteers' Inn in New Street. Next to it can be seen part of the brickwork of a building. The brickwork has 'blue-header' bricks often used in the 19th century for a decorative effect. The building has been demolished.

A view of New Street showing another inn – 'The Rose and Crown'. This later became 'The Greyhound' but now it is a shop.

'The New Inn', New Street. This was rebuilt in the standard mock-Tudor style of Maidstone brewing firm Style & Winch Ltd. Badly damaged in the air raid of 1943, it was finally demolished.

New Rents

This was a new development of the town in the 17th century. Only two buildings of any antiquity remain today. The two pictures below show buildings which have been demolished.

(a) Allen's House and Shop was in New Rents. The window display seems to consist entirely of oil lamps, a commodity much in demand. Note the oil drums outside.

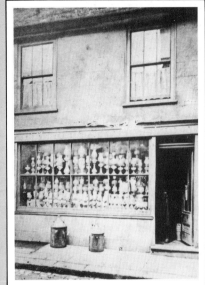

(a)

(b) All in this photograph, erected by George Lewis the draper.

Later, more imposing buildings were erected lower down New Rents and the firm became Lewis & Hyland's. In 1973 every building was demolished for redevelopment.

(b)

(c) The demolition of the old windmill which stood in Regent's Place. The Barns' album has a picture before the demolition, but so badly faded as to be incapable of restoration or reproduction.

(c)

24

The houses in Church Road were known as Church Villas. At the corner of Church Road and Elwick Road, 'The Cedars' was built for George Elliott in 1863. In modern times the house was used as offices for the Ashford Urban District Council.

The gardens of 'The Cedars' and a gardener's house were on the opposite side of Elwick Road. Later the gardens became part of a nursery. A warehouse now occupies the site.

This is a view of Elwick Road taken from the Market end. The houses were designed by a Tunbridge Wells architect, Willicombe, and erected for Elliott on land leased by George Elwick Jemmett. The original design of the gates should be noted.

Education
in Ashford

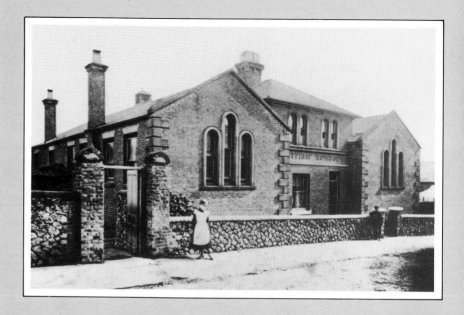

The British School was built in 1862 in West Street, closed in 1931 and became the Salvation Army Citadel.

The National School at Barrow Hill is now St. Mary's Primary School and was erected in 1841. Alexander Apsley of a prominent Ashford family designed it.

The Board School was erected in 1879 in Beaver Road at the corner of Victoria Road.

The Cemetery gatehouse in Canterbury Road, built in Victorian Golthic style. The cemetery was opened in 1860.

The photograph was taken from the old windmill in Regent's Place and described by Barns as a 'bird's eye view'. The Gothic style building in the centre was the Wesleyan Chapel in Hempstead Street (see page 21) and we are looking at the backs of the Bank Street shops.

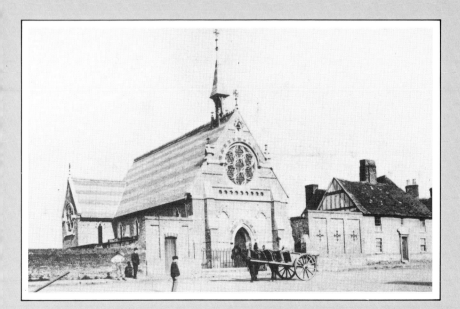

The Catholic Church no longer has the bell turret seen here and the houses on the right have gone. The church was built in 1865.

Beaver

The Avenue, Beaver Fields. This was probably in the area now occupied by Victoria Park.

A view of some of the earlier houses in Beaver Road on the east side. People are standing on the bridge over the culvert − still there.

Another peaceful scene and an aspect of the town from the south. The houses in Elwick Road and the Corn Exchange can be clearly identified. The latter was opened in 1861.

Mr. Reece's shop in Denmark Road,
South Ashford.

Mr. Denness's shop in South
Ashford.

Christ Church, South Ashford, built
for the growing population south of
the railway line.

Nostalgic

The Beaver Toll Gate which controlled the traffic on the turnpike road between Ham Street and Ashford. The gate was south of Christ Church which can be seen in the distance.

An uninterrupted view from Beaver Fields of the Corn Exchange and the market.

At the time of the photograph this was known as Bybrook Farm and the home of a Mr. Raysbrook. Later it was the home of Mr. A. G. Bailey, a coal merchant. Later it became the Bybrook Tavern and now part of the Post House Hotel.

East Stour Farm was at the end of the present day Mableden Avenue. It stood on the site of the ancient manor of Estewer mentioned in the Domesday Book.

This view looks towards a shadowy Ashford. The chimney stack on the horizon is probably the foundry. A peaceful scene.

Wellesley Villas was no doubt a classy development. Tutt was a nurseryman and later had nurseries at the corner of Elwick Road.

31

Rail & Gas

The South Eastern Railway Station which was built in 1865.

The Gas House in Gas Works Lane off Godinton Road. The Gas Works superceded the first works in Station Road on part of the present Car Park.

The Manager's House in Gas Works Lane.

Ashford West

The sanatorium in Warren Lane was given by Mr. Henry Whitfeld and opened in 1860.

The photograph does not show what the operation was, but we can surmise that the excavation was a cutting for the Maidstone to Ashford Railway which was built in 1884.

This is Barrow Hill House, now occupied by a veterinary practice. The house is much older than it appears externally and was once the home of a Dr. Jacob in the 17th century.

Beaver

The Old House, Beaver, known variously as Beavor House, Farm or Little Hampton. By the end of the 19th century it had become ruinous, was struck by lightning on 4th September 1903 and burnt down.

The name Beaver came from a Norman, John de Beavor, who was possessed of the land in the 12th century. There is no connection with the name of the animal. John was no doubt one of the Conqueror's men who came from a place Beauvoir (fine view). The house originally dated from the 14th century (or earlier) and was quite magnificent in its timbering. There were marble floors (Bethersden marble?) and contained a chapel, leading some to think that there was some religious connection. There is no evidence for this. Wealthy people often had their own private chapels.

An oriel window at the 14th century Old House at Beaver.

(a)

(c)

(b)

(d)

(e)

Appledore has seen several changes in its fortunes. A Saxon town and seaport, it prospered with fleets of ships sailing up to its very doorsteps – a rather mixed blessing when the Danes ravaged it in AD 892 with a fleet of 250 ships. All prosperity dwindled when the River Rother changed course and left it stranded. In the Middle Ages the Horne family held sway over the district. Robert Horne was a friend of Ashford's Sir John Fogge. In the 18th century Appledore was described as having mean houses occupied by graziers and smugglers!

(a) Horne's Place Chapel, erected by Sir William Horne in 1366. The photograph shows the west doorway, which was originally approached by stone steps and the entry to the crypt.

(b) Another picture of Horne's Place Chapel which has been restored now by the Department of the Environment and is open to the public. The large east window, shown bricked up, has now been glazed. The ladder was removed and the window with the door restored.

(c) The tower is no longer clothed in the disfiguring ivy which here conceals interesting architectural features such as some unusual belfry windows.

(d) The Street from Avery's.

(e) Mr. Sim's shop.

(a)

(a) The Swan Inn. The building shown in the photograph was demolished in 1910 and the present hotel erected in its place.

(b)

(c)

(b) Mr. Spilstead's Drawing Room showing a good example of a Victorian furnished interior.

(d)

(c) Sheep shearing at Mr. Spilstead's.

(d) Another picture of Mr. Spilstead's room. Note the clock under a glass dome and the epergne, a Victorian favourite.

(e)

(e) Mr. Spilstead's house with its quaint summerhouse — and more ivy.

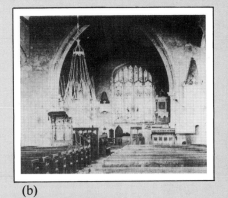

(a)

(b)

(a) Biddenden. The Church from the west. In comparison with similar Kentish towers this one's top-heavy battlements spoil the effect.

(b) Biddenden Church interior.

(c)

(c) Biddenden. The photographer just calls these 'Old Houses'. These were clothworkers' houses and workshops, now called 'The Old Cloth Hall' and date from the 16th century.

(d)

(d) Bilsington Church. This quaint little church overlooking Romney Marsh looks much the same today as over a hundred years ago when the photograph was taken. There is much Norman work with later details.

(e)

(e) Bilsington. Seeley's House. Note the ragstone wall.

(f)

(f) Bilsington. The obelisk was erected in memory of Sir William Cosway, M.P. for Kent and owner of Bilsington killed by falling from a stage coach in 1835. The monument was struck by lightning in recent years.

Godinton

(a) Godinton House, Great Chart. This shows the north front built about 1800 that imitates the main front with its shaped gables, which incidentally were popularised at Knole Park.

(b) Godinton Park. The Avenue. A beautifully composed photograph.

(c) Godinton Park. A great oak.

(d) Godinton Park. The Lodge Gate near Potter's Corner. The shaped gables repeat those seen at the mansion and also in the village of Great Chart.

(e) Godinton House, Great Chart. The great mansion was built by Nicholas Toke in 1622, but there are older parts within. This general view of the house before the clipped yew hedges seen today which were the work of Sir Reginald Blomfield, the well-known architect, in 1902.

(f) Godinton Park. A camp for Volunteers. The Tokes, the owners had military connections.

(g) Godinton Park. A great oak seen in the winter snow.

(a)

(b)

(a) Godinton House. The fireplace in the Drawing Room. Carved Bethersden marble is much in evidence.

(b) Godinton House. The fireplace in the Library.

(c)

(d)

(c) Godinton House. Part of the Hall with its rich furnishings. Notice the huge hanging lantern and the fireplace with its carved overmantel. The roof timbering shows that this was part of the medieval house.

(d) Godinton House. Anne Boleyn's Cabinet.

Great Chart

Great Chart is said to have been older than Ashford. It was of some importance with a market place with a number of wealthy and important people living within the parish. There were of course the Tokes of Godinton, the Engehams of Singleton and the Goldwells. James Goldwell of Great Chart became Bishop of Norwich.

(a)

(a) A fine photograph of this interesting church at Great Chart.

(b) The Church interior showing the organ at that time situated at the west end.

(b)

(c)

(c) The interior of the Church as it appeared to Mr. Barns in the 1880's.

(d) The so-called 'Pest House' in the churchyard at Great Chart. The name is probably a corruption of the words Priest House.

(d)

(e)

(e) A house in the Street. Behind the Georgian frontage there is a medieval house. The owners pose for the photographer and the boy on the right watches him in action.

(a)

(a) Court Lodge, Great Chart. This is the west front of a remarkable 13th century important building. The house is stone built which is rare in these parts.

(b)

(c)

(b) Court Lodge, Great Chart. The porch doorway which dates from circa 1300.

(c) The Friars, an 18th century house, now the home of the Friars School.

(d)

(d) A closer view of the village Street showing the village shop and some houses with gables in a similar style to those of Godinton House. Further on is the Swan Inn.

(e) The Street looking towards Ashford and the crossroads.

(e)

(f)

(f) Great Chart. A similar view to (e) but nearer to the crossroads. The Swan Inn shows the position.

Great Chart

(a) At the crossroads with the Smithy on the right at the corner of Ninn Lane.

(b) The Street looking towards Ashford with the Black Dog Inn on the left.

(c) Looking from Godinton Park towards Great Chart Parish Church in the distance.

(d) The entrance to the Street as seen coming from Ashford. The fine avenue of trees on the right is no longer there.

(e) The entrance to Godinton Park looking towards the village. The large trees are no more.

(a)

(b)

(c)

(d)

(e)

(a)

(c)

(b)

(d)

(e)

(a) Singleton Manor, Great Chart. The interior of the Great Hall of the fine moated Manor House dating from the 15th century. The plaster ceiling was inserted in the late 16th century.

(b) Singleton Manor, Great Chart. This is the rear view of the great moated Manor House. On the right there is a modern structure but in the middle is one of the windows of the Hall. The flowerbed in the middle hides the ancient well. The smaller gable on the right, seen above the bush, is the roof of the stair turret built after the hall was floored over.

(c) Yardhurst. A gable with its intricately carved barge boards – a later addition to the main building – 17th century.

(d) Yardhurst, just within the parish near Daniel's Water. The building is of the type known as Wealden in which the central hall section is recessed, the continuous eaves supported by curved braces. 15th century.

(e) Little London. This ancient building was described by the photographer as in Great Chart, but in fact it was within the boundaries of the parish of Ashford. It was situated on the road to Great Chart and was demolished by the Council when it developed the Industrial Estate. It was built in the 14th century and later converted into two cottages.

Little Chart

(a)

(a) Little Chart Church. Alas, only the tower stands today. The church was largely destroyed by a Flying Bomb in the last war. A new church was built nearer to the village.

(b)

(c)

(b) The Paper Mills situated on the Great Stour famous at one time for handmade paper but latterly for flong.

(c) Calehill House, the ancestral home of the Darells, was a rather stark Georgian mansion. This picture shows the front elevation.

(d)

(d) Calehill House viewed from the lawn side with little to relieve the monotony of the architecture.

(e) Calehill House. The 'Grotto'. How the Victorians loved these sham features. Note the rustic flower stands.

(e)

(f) Calehill Park. This picture shows the 'Ruins' in the Park. The window shows that here was the medieval house of the Darells, demolished when the Georgian mansion was built.

(f)

(a)

(b)

(a) One of the Darell monuments. The Darells were an ancient family who owned Calehill House.

(b) The monument to Sir Robert Darell and his wife with the figures of their nine children below.

(c) Calehill Park. Mr. Wise and daughters pose for the photographer beside an ornamental stone flower urn.

(c)

(d)

(d) Calehill Park. Unnamed people (probably Darells) survey the Park from the Terrace.

(e)

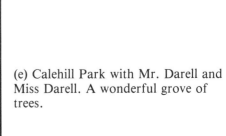

(e) Calehill Park with Mr. Darell and Miss Darell. A wonderful grove of trees.

Brabourne

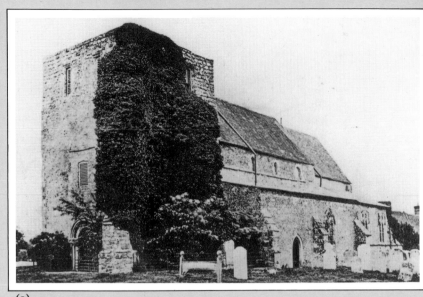
(a)

(a) Brabourne Church. Another great tower like Brook's, disfigured by the ubiquitous ivy.

(b) Brabourne Church. The small Norman doorway.

(b)

(c)

(c) Brabourne Church. A typical medieval porch.

Mersham

(d) Mersham. The monument to Bridget, Lady Knatchbull, wife of Sir Norton Knatchbull. The sculptor was Nicholas Stone the King's sculptor who was paid £30 for his work in 1626.

(d)